TopReaders

Things with Wings

Denise Ryan

Contents

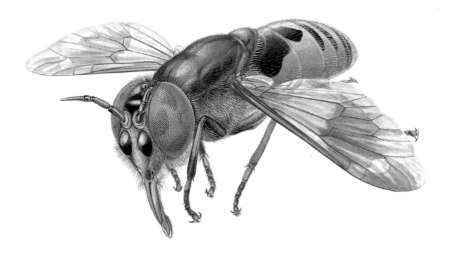

Birds, insects, and some other animals have wings. Most of them fly, but some of them don't. You can find out about things with wings in this book.

How Birds Fly

Birds are covered with light, strong feathers. Their bodies are like flying machines.

wings up

wings down and back

Birds have light bones and strong muscles to help them fly.

light bones

strong muscles

wings down

ready to start again

Eagles

Eagles are large birds of prey.
They have hooked bills,
sharp eyes, and powerful talons.

hooked bill
_____

talon
_____

Bald eagles live in North America.
They swoop from the sky to catch fish
and ducks.

sharp eye

bald eagle

Geese

Some kinds of geese are long-distance travelers. They breed in the north and then fly south for the winter.

barnacle geese

Barnacle geese fly in groups.
The birds make the shape
of a letter V as they fly.

Weavers

Weavers work in groups to make their nests. Male birds put strips of grass and leaves together to build a nest shaped like a basket with a roof.

Female weavers look after the eggs and chicks.

weavers building their nests

Penguins

Penguins are birds that cannot fly.
They use their wings as flippers
when they swim underwater.

jackass penguin

royal penguin

adelie penguin

king penguin

snares penguin

emperor penguin

Penguins spend some of their life on land and some in the water. They live in the most southern part of the world.

Butterflies

Butterflies have four wings.
They are covered with tiny scales
that give the butterfly its bright colors.

lacewing
butterfly

Butterflies flutter from flower to flower.
They feed on nectar inside the flower.

Flies

Flies have two wings. They have to work hard to fly. Their wings go up and down very quickly. Flies move their legs backward and forward, too.

wings down

wings up

wings out

legs forward

legs backward

If you don't like flies in your house,
ask some spiders to move in.
Spiders love to eat flies!

Fireflies

Fireflies are small beetles.
They contact each other by flashing
a yellow or green light.

female firefly

male firefly

Male fireflies flash light as they fly overhead. Females flash back from the ground.

Dragonflies

Dragonflies have two pairs of strong, see-through wings and a long, narrow body. They are usually found around lakes, ponds, streams, and wetlands.

dragonfly

see-through wing

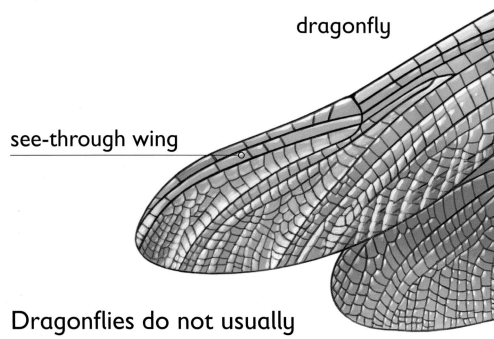

Dragonflies do not usually sting humans, although they will bite if they need to escape.

long, narrow body

Wasps

Wasps are yellow with black markings. Their bright colors warn other animals that they are dangerous.

see-through wing

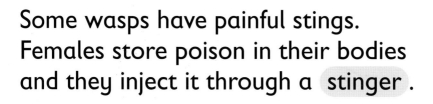

Some wasps have painful stings. Females store poison in their bodies and they inject it through a stinger .

wasp

black spot

poison

stinger

Bats

Bats are the only mammals that fly. They sleep during the day and fly at night when they go hunting. Some bats eat fruit, but most eat insects.

bats flying at night

Bats send out high-pitched sounds that bounce off things around them. The echoes help them work out where things are.

Flying Squirrels

Flying squirrels move through
the air without wings.
They glide from one tree
to another.

Flying squirrels have webs of furry skin.
They are like parachutes and help them
to fall slowly and safely.

flying squirrel

web of
furry skin

Archaeopteryx

Archaeopteryx lived about 160 million years ago. It is sometimes called "the first bird." It was about the size of a crow and had feathers and wings.

feathers

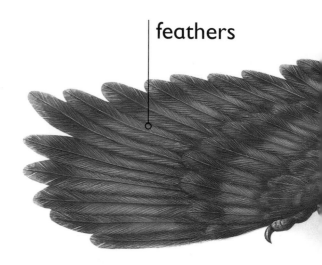

Archaeopteryx could fly but its wings were not very strong.

wing

dragonfly

Archaeopteryx swooping
on a dragonfly

Quiz

Can you match each animal with its name?

dragonfly   penguin

eagle   wasp

Glossary

birds of prey: birds that hunt animals for food

breed: to produce young

echoes: sounds that are repeated

flippers: parts of an animal that help it to swim

flutter: to move quickly and lightly

mammals: animals that drink milk from their mother's body when they are babies

nectar: a sweet liquid inside some flowers

stinger: the part of an insect that passes poison to another animal

talons: claws, especially on birds of prey

weavers: birds that make a nest by joining grass and leaves

Index